PHOTOGRAPHY YEARBOOK 1996

INTERNATIONALES JAHRBUCH DER FOTOGRAPHIE 1996

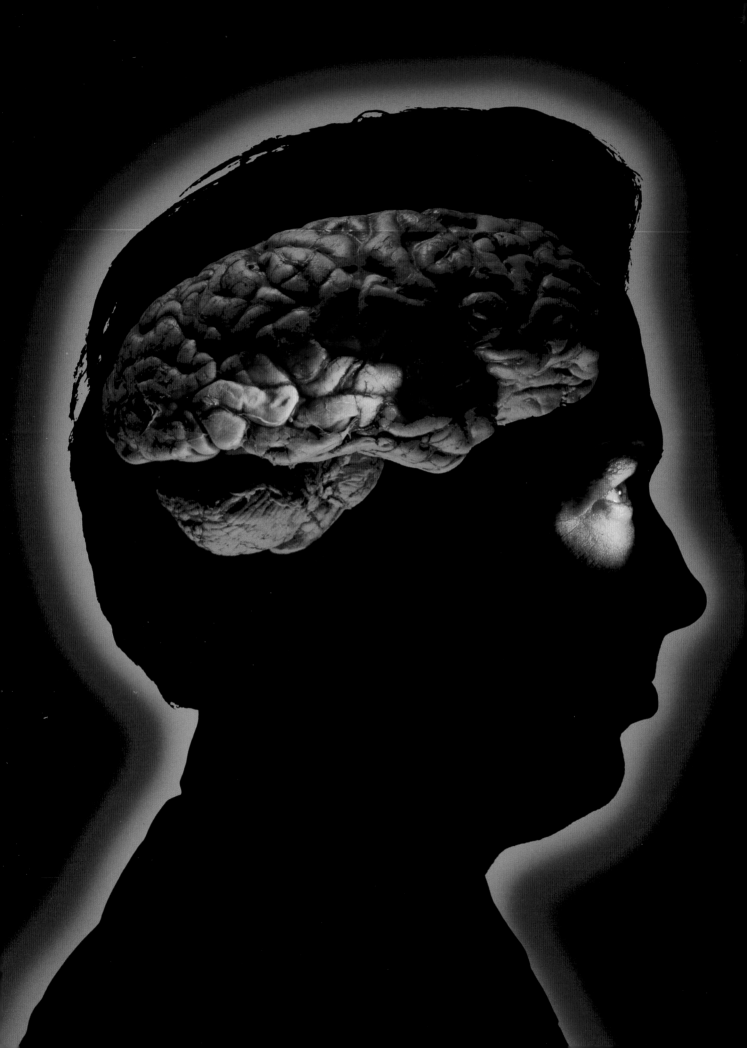

PHOTOGRAPHY YEARBOOK 1996

INTERNATIONALES JAHRBUCH DER FOTOGRAPHIE 1996

Joseph Meehan
EDITOR

Chris Hinterobermaier
CONTRIBUTING EDITOR

Grant Bradford
DESIGNER

FOUNTAIN PRESS

PUBLISHED BY
FOUNTAIN PRESS LIMITED
FOUNTAIN HOUSE
2 GLADSTONE ROAD
KINGSTON-UPON-THAMES
SURREY KT1 3HD

© FOUNTAIN PRESS 1995
ISBN 0 86343 302 2

EDITOR
JOSEPH MEEHAN

CONTRIBUTING EDITOR
CHRIS HINTEROBERMAIER

DESIGNER
GRANT BRADFORD

REPRODUCTION & PRINTING
REGENT PUBLISHING
SERVICES LTD

Deutsche Ausgabe
© 1995 WILHELM KNAPP VERLAG,
Neiderlassung der Droste Verlag GmbH,
Düsseldorf

Photograph opposite title page
TIM VERNON
United Kingdom
Medical Illustration/St. James's Hospital Trust

CONTENTS

EDITOR'S MESSAGE

This is my first issue as Editor of the Photography Yearbook though it is certainly not my first experience with yearbooks having contributed to others as a photographer as well as serving as a judge and contributing editor. Those of you who saw last year's issue of the Yearbook will know I also wrote the retrospective for that 60th anniversary volume. Researching that overview by going back through every page of every volume since 1935 had a profound effect on my perception of the Yearbook giving me a deep appreciation of its historical role in chronicling the evolution of photography in the modern era.

In my research I paid particular attention to the articles that used to appear by photographers and how these documented the development of photographic style, technique and technology in a very personal way. Also of special significance to me were statements made by past editors who invariably reiterated the goals of the Yearbook and described how they were carrying out those goals. Most also commented on the "state of photography" as they saw it reflected in the changes in photographic equipment as well as the content and quality of the submissions.

As a continuance of these practices, I too would like to begin my message by reiterating the views of past editors and state that the overall purpose of the Photography Yearbook is to bring together each year in one volume, the very best in international photography.

In a practical sense, however, the quality of the images in the Yearbook and the degree to which they are representative of photography internationally, are dependent upon the submissions we receive. My research indicated that, compared to earlier editions, the range of countries and number of photographers outside the UK has decreased noticeably in the past decade. Consequently, one of my goals as editor will be to cast an even wider net from which to draw contributors by working to increase the awareness of our publication worldwide. To that end, I welcome the assistance of Dr. Chris Hinterobermaier of Austria, who is a contributing editor for this 1996 issue. In addition to being a fine photographer in his own right, Chris has traveled all over the world, serving as a judge in a wide variety of international competitions. He is also a prime mover in the Austrian Super Circuit which is an annual international photographic competition of emerging importance in Austria.

Another goal for the Yearbook will be to return to some of the formats that have been so successful in past volumes. This is partly an acknowledgment that the Photography Yearbook is the most unique publication of its kind in the world today. Over its 60 year history, it has not only accepted work for publication by some of the world's finest photographers such as Man Ray, Yousuf Karsh, Andreas Feininger, Alfred Eisenstaedt, Henri Cartier-Bresson, W. Eugene Smith, Edward Weston, Paul Strand, Bill Brandt and Cecil Beaton, but it has also singled out such artists in special features. This practice returns with the 1996 volume in individual sections on the work of the Czech photographer, Miloslav Stibor and the late Pedro Luis Raota of Argentinia; both considered legends in their respective countries. From the UK comes Wildlife photographer of the Year, Martyn Colbeck and from Russia the dynamic work of Vladimir Vitov, while one of the acknowledged masters of American fashion and beauty photography, Robert Farber, completes this selection.

It also has to be acknowledged that photography is rapidly changing in both the equipment used to make pictures as well as in the pictorial content itself. New techniques and advances in technology are nothing new for photography, but in this decade before the turn of the millennium, the degree of change and the speed at which it is taking place is unprecedented. As an international publication with a long history of documenting changes in photography, we will be returning to another past practice. Namely, to address more fully, the "state of photography." We will begin this with a special section entitled; "The Electronic Photography Revolution: Where Do We Stand Today?" to help photographers understand this new technology and to consider its more controversial aspects. Accordingly, this section also contains a complete statement of the Yearbook's position regarding the electronic image.

Finally, there is the past practice of the Editor commenting, in general, on photography as a medium and what they look for in submissions. Invariably, these comments were a reflection of the editor's experiences in the field. In my case, those experiences have come from more than 25 years in photography, including a broad-based commercial business that encompasses everything from action and landscape photography to studio portraits and product work. There have also been many years of teaching photography in the United States, Great Britain and Asia, and the publication of hundreds of articles in photographic magazines as well as ten books on photographic techniques. All these experiences have opened my eyes wide to the enormous range of expression that exists in this medium giving me an appreciation of photography as a diverse and personal medium of expression.

Photography is truly the most universal language available to people around the world today, transcending the written and spoken word because it does not suffer from the limitations of translation or dialectic interpretations. Even music, so long touted as "the universal language" should really be considered second to photography if we think for a moment about how many people take photographs as opposed to playing a musical instrument.

Every second of everyday, millions of professional and amateur photographers all over the world are recording, with the click of a shutter, the people, places and events of the world for anyone to see. Many of these photographers have chosen to use the camera to interpret their views of life's eternal themes such as beauty, love and conflict. It is those photographs and their creators who interest us the most, for they are using this medium to interpret reality in some personal way. This often separates the photographer as artist from those who just record what is there, illustrating again the conclusions of that shrewd observer of human behavior, Oscar Wilde: *"Art is the most intense mode of individualism that the world has known."*

It is this individual view of the world that interests us most as chroniclers of international photography because it honours one of the main functions of photography put into words many years ago by Edward Steichen, that photography *"is a major force in explaining man to man."* Anyone who has taken the time to look at a large body of photographs has learned that it is those pictures that force the observer to react in some way, that are the ones that remain in our memories, invariably producing more of an awareness, understanding or appreciation of the subject in the photograph. We learn from such pictures because they have shown us the world in a way that we have missed or at least not paid attention to. These are "successful pictures" and the best of them are photography's examples of what Oscar Wilde meant when he said: *"No great artist sees things as they really are. If he did he would cease to be an artist."*

For some, a photograph must conform to a proscribed notion of a "balanced composition" or a "correctly executed" technique and once this is done, they feel secure to then decide on the worth of the photograph in terms of its subject matter. There is a fine and honoured tradition that has given (and undoubtedly will continue to give) photography some of its most beautiful and stirring images. Other observers, however, will be able to see a raw value in visual expressions that are not grounded in the recognized conventions. Such photographs are often more expressions of energy and emotions than line or form. I see the value of both of these approaches and will not hesitate to display both side by side. For I believe that the Yearbook must preserve and perpetuate the traditions of photographic expression while encouraging the new, whatever that may turn out to be. In this sense, the Yearbook should never find itself playing the same role as the Beaux Arts group who, in their official position as purveyors of the arts, year after year rejected and insulted what is now acknowledged as the magnificent work of Renoir, Monet and the other Impressionist painters.

Here, we would be well guided by the words of Alfred North Whitehead: *"Art flourishes where there is a sense of adventure, a sense of nothing having been done before, of complete freedom to experiment; but when caution comes in you get repetition, and repetition is the death of art."* Thus, in the end, we can only say that the Photography Yearbook does not come with a guarantee to please its readers, but rather with a pledge to chronicle the best it has seen each year.

Joseph Meehan
EDITOR

VORWORT

Dies ist mein erstes Jahr als Redakteur des **Internationalen Jahrbuchs der Fotografie,** aber allerdings nicht meine erste Erfahrung mit der Herausgabe eines Jahrbuchs. Ich habe zu vergangenen Jahrbüchern nicht nur als Fotograf beigetragen, sondern auch in der Eigenschaft als Juror und Mitredakteur gewirkt. Ebenso verfasste ich die Retrospektive für die Ausgabe zum 60 jährigen Jubiläum des **Jahrbuchs.** In meiner Vorbereitung für das Jubiläum schaute ich mir jede Seite in jedem Jahrbuch an, und dies hinterließ einen unheimlichen Eindruck auf mich. Ich erkannte daß das Jahrbuch eine geschichtliche Rolle spielt als Chronik der Entwicklung der Fotografie.

Ich las die Artikel, die von Fotografen geschrieben waren, mit besonderem Interesse, da sie auf sehr persönliche Weise die Entwicklung von fotografischem Stil, Methode und Technik dokumentierten. Mit demselben Interesse schaute ich mir die Kommentare von früheren Redakteuren an, die ausnahmslos das ursprüngliche Ziel des **Jahrbuchs** darlegten und beschrieben wie sie versuchten dieses Ziel zu erreichen. Viele erläuterten auch den Stand der Fotografie der sich, in ihrer Meinung, in den Veränderungen der fotografischen Ausrüstungen und in dem Inhalt und der Qualität der eingesendeten Bilder wiederspiegelte.

Um diese Tradition fortzuführen, möchte ich auch zu Anfang meines Vorworts die Meinung der früheren Redakteure wiederholen, und sagen daß der grundsätzliche Zweck des **Internationalen Jahrbuchs der Fotografie** ist, jedes Jahr die Besten von internationalen Aufnahmen in einem Band anzusammeln.

Das mag in der Theorie richtig sein, aber in der Praxis hängt die Qualität der Bilder (und ob sie auch tatsächlich eine internationale Ansammlung darstellen) von den Einsendungen ab. Es fiel mir auf, daß die Anzahl von vertretenen Ländern und Fotografen ausserhalb Englands in dem letzten Jahrzehnt ständig abgenommen hat. Infolgedessen, als Redakteur, möchte ich ein grösseres Netz ausspannen und unsere Publikation weltweit bekannt machen, um hoffentlich mehr Einsendungen zu erhalten. Mit diesem Ziel vor Augen ist der Beitrag des Herrn Dr. Chris Hinterobermaier von Österreich, der Mitredakteur für diese 1996 Auflage ist, sehr begrüßenswert. Erstmals ist Chris selbst ein ausgezeichneter Fotograf und hat ausserdem in der ganzen Welt an den verschiedensten internationalen Wettbewerben als Juror teilgenommen. Er ist auch einer der Verantwortlichen für den österreichischen Super Circuit, ein jährlicher Wettbewerb in Österreich von zunehmender Bedeutung.

Ein weiteres Ziel für das **Jahrbuch** ist einige der in der Vergangenheit erfolgreichen Features wieder anzubieten. Es ist in Anerkennung, daß das **Jahrbuch** heutzutage eine einzigartige Publikation in der Welt ist. Während der letzten 60 Jahre hat das **Jahrbuch** nicht nur die Fotografien von solch berühmten Fotografen wie Man Ray, Yousuf Karsh, Andreas Feininger, Alfred Eisenstaedt, Henri Cartier-Bresson, W. Eugene Smith, Edward Weston, Paul Strand, Bill Brandt and Cecil Beaton veröffentlicht, sondern hat auch die Künstler selbst in besonderen Features vorgestellt. Wir wollen diesen Brauch in der 1996 Ausgabe weiterführen, mit Einzelteilen über den Tschechen Miloslav Stibor und den verstorbenen Pedro Luis Raota von Argentinien. Beide sind in ihren Heimatländern als legendär anerkannt. Von England kommt der Naturfotograf des Jahres, Martyn Colbeck; von Rußland die dynamischen Aufnahmen des Vladimir Vitoffs, und von Amerika einer der anerkannten Meister der Mode und Schönheitsfotografie, Robert Farber.

Es muß auch darauf hingewiesen werden wie rapide sich die Fotografie verändert, und zwar nicht nur was die Apparate und den Zubehör anbetrifft die jetzt zur Verfügung stehen, aber auch die Themen die in den Bildern dargestellt werden. Neue Methoden und technische Entwicklungen per se sind nichts Neues in der Fotografie, aber in diesem Jahrzehnt vor dem neuen Millennium, die Entwicklungen und die Geschwindigkeit mit der sie vor sich gehen ist unheimlich und ist beispiellos. Als internationale Publikation, mit einer langen Vergangenheit die Veränderungen in der Fotografie zu dokumentieren, werden wir auch wieder zu diesem Brauch zurückkehren. Nämlich, den neuesten Stand der Fotografie näher zu erläutern. Dies wird in dem Teil "The Electronic Photography Revolution: Where do We Stand Today?" behandelt mit dem Ziel im Auge diese neue Technologie zu erklären, so daß Fotografen diese Entwicklungen verstehen und gleicherzeit einen Einblick in die Kontroversen, die daraus erstanden sind, gewinnen. Dementsprechend befindet sich in diesem Teil auch der Standpunkt des **Jahrbuchs** was elektronische Aufnahmen anbetrifft.

Und, letztens, frühere Redakteure haben immer Bemerkungen im allgemeinen über das Thema Fotografie gemacht, was sie bedeutet als Medium, und welche Fotos erwünscht sind. Selbstverständlich waren diese Kommentare gefärbt mit den individuellen fotografischen Erlebnissen. Ich selber habe meine Erfahrungen mit diesem Medium über mehr als 25 Jahre gesammelt, und fotografiere beruflich vielvältige Motive, unter anderen Sport, Landschaften, Porträts, Stilleben und verschiedenste Produkte für Werbenmaterial. Ausserdem habe ich viele Jahre in Amerika, England und Asien Fotografie unterrichtet, und habe hunderte von Artikeln für Fotomagazine geschrieben und zehn Bücher an Fototechnik. Durch all dies habe ich gesehen wie viele Ausdrucksstile in diesem Medium existieren, und ich habe erkannt, daß diese Kunst ein vielseitiges und persönliches Ausdrucksmedium ist.

Fotografie is doch die wahre, weltweite Universalsprache, und als solche tranzendiert sie das geschriebene sowie das gesprochene Wort, denn sie benötigt keine Übersetzung und ist in jedem Dialekt klar zu verstehen. Sogar Musik, die man immer als die "Universalsprache" anerkannt hat, kommt nicht mit der Fotografie mit, wenn man bedenkt wieviel Menschen Bilder aufnehmen und wieviele ein musikalisches Instrument spielen.

Überall, millionen von Professionellen und Amateuren dokumentieren in jeder Sekunde und an jedem Tag, mit dem Druck auf den Auslöser die Menschen, Umgebungen und Ereignisse ihrer Umwelt für Alle zu sehen, zu erkennen und zu erfassen. Viele dieser Fotografen haben die Kamera gewählt um die ewigen Themen des Lebens wie Schönheit, Liebe und Konflikt zu interpretieren. Dies sind die Bilder, sowie deren Fotografen, die uns am meisten interessieren, denn sie benutzen das Medium um Realität auf persönliche Weise darzustellen. Dies verwandelt den Fotograf zum Künstler und trennt ihn von denjenigen die einfach knipsen was sie vor Augen haben. Wie Oscar Wilde es schon vor langem sehr scharfsinnig bemerkte: *"Kunst ist die intensivste Art des Individualismus in der Welt."*

Es ist diese individuelle Interpretation der Welt die uns in unserer Rolle als Chronisten der internationalen Fotografie am meisten interessiert, weil sie einer der Hauptaufgaben des Mediums Ehre macht, wie es Edward Steichen vor vielen Jahren gesagt hat, daß Fotografie *"eine bedeutende Rolle spielt um Mensch zu Mensch zu erklären."* Jeder der sich Zeit nimmt und viele Aufnahmen anschaut, weiß es sind diejenigen Bilder die eine Reaktion in uns hevorrufen, die sich als ein visuelles Erlebnis einprägen, und die uns näher an das Subjekt heranbringen. Wir lernen von solchen Bildern, denn sie zeigen uns einen Ausschnitt des Daseins den wir bisher nicht auf diese Art und Weise gesehen haben. Das sind "erfolgreiche Bilder", und die Besten von diesen sind Beispiele von Oscar Wildes Behauptung: *"Ein wahrer Künstler sieht nicht wie Dinge wirklich sind. Sieht er sie auf diese Weise, hört er auf Künstler zu sein."*

Manche Leute sind der Meinung, daß ein Foto sich allen Regeln der "ausgeglichenen Bildgestaltung" anpassen muß, oder daß die angewandte Technik "akkurat" sein muß. Nur dann, glauben sie, kann man den Wert des Bildthemas entscheiden. Dieser Standpunkt repräsentiert die langwährige Tradition die einige der besten Bilder in dem Kunstbereich der Fotografie produziert hat (und ohne Zweifel so tun wird in der Zukunft). Andere Beobachter, auf der anderen Seite, sind fähig einen grundsätzlichen Wert in solch visuellen Ausdrücken, die nicht im traditionellen Stil gemacht wurden, zu erkennen. Solche Aufnahmen sind oft Ausdrücke von Energie und Gefühlen und nicht Wiederspiegelungen von Linie und Form. Meiner Meinung nach sind beide Ausdrucksweisen gerechtfertigt und ich werde sie ohne Zögern nebeneinander darstellen. Denn ich glaube daß das **Jahrbuch** die Traditionen des Fotografieausdrucks aufrechterhalten muß, und zur gleichen Zeit neue künstlerische Ausdrücke fördern soll. In diesem Sinn soll das **Jahrbuch** nie denselben Fehler wie die Beaux Arts Gruppe machen, die in ihrer Rolle as offizielle Hüter der Künste, Jahr für Jahr, die heutzutage anerkannten, hervorragenden Werke von Renoir, Monet und den anderen Impressionisten beleidigt und abgehnt haben.

Es wäre besser die Worte von Alfred North whitehead zu Herzen zu nehmen :*"Mit Abenteuerlust gedeiht die Kunst; die Idee daß etwas noch nie vorher versucht wurde; die Idee in völliger Freiheit zu experimentieren. Geht man mit Vorsicht daran, wiederholt man sich, und Wiederholung tötet die Kunst."* So, letzten Endes, können wir nicht garantieren daß das **Jahrbuch** jedem Leser gefallen wird, aber es verpflichtet sich jährlich die besten Aufnahmen die uns gesendet werden in der Chronik einzutragen.

Joseph Meehan
HERAUSGEBER

The ELECTRONIC PHOTOGRAPHY Revolution

Where do we stand today?

JOSEPH MEEHAN

We are in the midst of the most significant revolution in photographic technology since the very invention of the medium itself. The ability to create and modify still pictures electronically is not only altering how photographs are being made and used, but this new technology is also challenging many of photography's most basic tenets, including calling into question the very definition of what is a photograph?

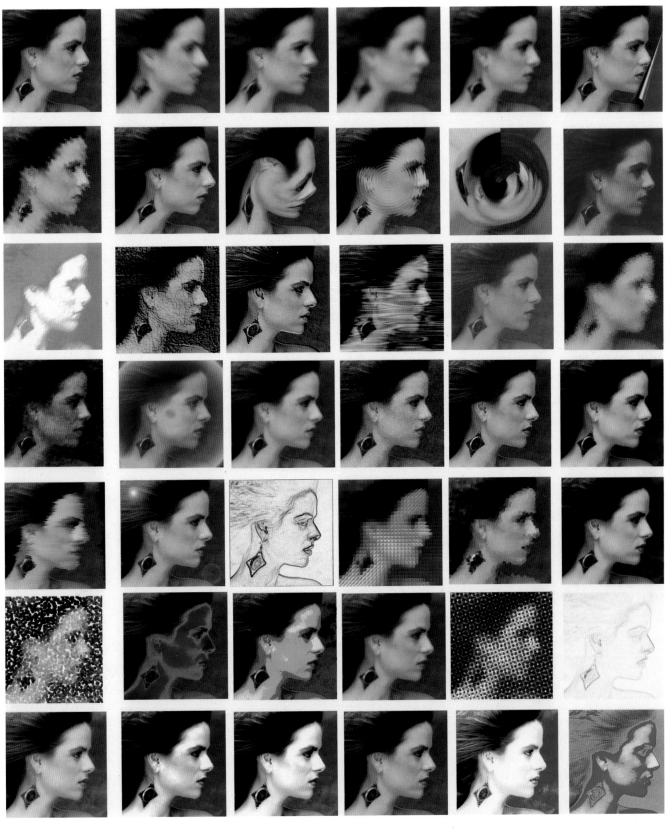

The power of various software
programs such as PhotoShop by
Adobe gives the person in front of
the computer enormous power to
completely change an image.
For example, here are just some of
the variations in an original portrait
(top left) that were done by
American photographer Tim
Morrissey using just the special
'filters' available in the PhotoShop
program. (Demonstration
photograph by Tim Morrissey,
Thermal Dye Transfer print)

We are in the midst of the most significant revolution in photographic technology since the very invention of the medium itself. The ability to create and modify still pictures electronically is not only altering how photographs are being made and used, but this new technology is also challenging many of photography's most basic tenets, including calling into question the very definition of what is a photograph?

In short, today's photographer is being offered electronic equipment that provides virtually total control over the image once it has been placed into the computer and what happens to that picture when it leaves the computer. For example, electronic based photography has opened up new methods of retouching, correction and altering picture content as well as providing for the production of electronically generated prints and transparencies. Pictures can be stored on tape or disks to be recalled and then duplicated 'endlessly' without any loss in quality. Images can even be transmitted from the computer over phone lines and other telecommunication routes as computer data for use by anyone who has the appropriate equipment to receive and reconstruct them.

In one way or another, all photographers will have to confront the enormous changes being brought about by this revolution and as chroniclers of trends and developments of photography worldwide, the **Photography Yearbook** is also concerned with the issues being raised by these changes.

WHY ELECTRONIC IMAGING IS A REVOLUTION

The most advanced products now available in electronic based imaging rely on the use of electronic devices that record light through the activation of millions of tiny contact points on a light sensitive surface or CCD (Charge Coupled Device). These points are translated into proportional visual representations of the scene called pixels (picture elements) in a process, not unlike the construction of a mosaic picture, known as digitalization.

Existing pictures can be placed into the computer either by scanning prints or transparencies with CCD equipped scanning devices, or an 'all electronic image' can be produced by using cameras equipped with CCD chips to take the picture initially. All this 'captured' light information is then processed by software in the computer which, on command, reconstructs the original, literally, pixel by pixel.

At first glance, it may seem that the construction of a picture from tiny elements is similar to the way individual photosensitive grains of silver halide react to light on film to form a picture. That given these similarities, the electronic revolution is more like a logical evolution in equipment that we have seen before as Super-8mm film was replaced by the video camera. But there are several important differences which really make this form of picture taking revolutionary and have caused controversy among photographers.

First of all, film captures the scene *en masse* in a single exposure appearing as a complete, continuous tone or 'analog' image. As the tiny grains of photosensitive materials react within the emulsion (first during exposure and then development), a picture emerges with seamless changes in the hues of colour and among the tones that fill-in and surround the specific shapes and contours of the subjects in the scene.

By contrast, in a digital image, the picture is made up of electronically separated pixel elements which can be controlled individually by sophisticated computer software such as Photoshop or Livepicture. This allows the photographer to change any part of the picture by using various computer commands that, in effect, alter each of these

The Digital Loop
Digital photography follows the same basic stages of production as does conventional photography but with the use of electronic recordings or a combination of conventional and digital methods. In the initial picture taking stage (capture), either an electronic camera is used to take the image or a conventional film/print is scanned into the computer. At this point, (electronic darkroom) the procedures are very similar to a conventional darkroom in the sense that the image is 'developed' by appearing on the computer screen where software programs can be used to alter it and store the final results. Finally in the last stage (output) a number of choices present themselves. Either a hard copy print can be made using conventional or electronic printers; or the data can remain in its digital form to be transported over telephone wires to another location or sent in some sort of storage form such as on disk, directly to a publisher for use in a book or magazine.

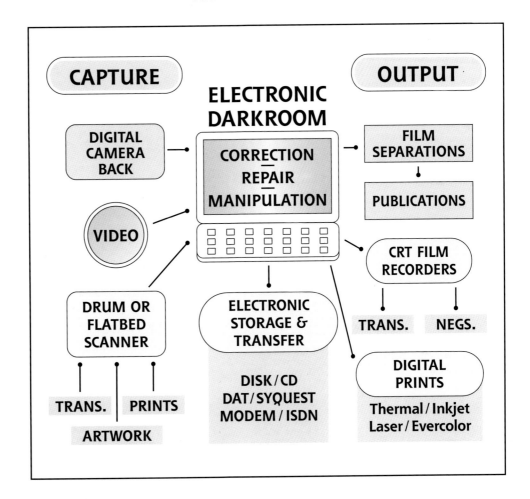

separate pixels. Thus, not only can such general characteristics as brightness, colour balance, hue and tone be controlled over an extremely wide range (far more than can ever be done with film), but the largest or smallest detail of line, form and shape can also be changed or even eliminated from the picture.

One very practical outcome of all this control is to make the tedious job of retouching flaws such as the removal of dust spots, skin imperfections, or the repair of scratches and even tears in a print or transparency, a relatively easy process. In addition, many more types of correction, previously impossible, are now a matter of just a few keystrokes on the computer.

Other corrective procedures common in photography such as altering contrast, brightness and correcting colour balance are easily accomplished on computer screens instead of having to go through the stages of reprinting or duping with filters or special films. While some photographers may be uncomfortable with the use of electronic methods to do these corrective procedures, most see them as remarkable and much appreciated advancements which can often save a 'beyond repair' print or transparency.

The real controversial aspect of digital photography, however, has emerged out of its ability to go well beyond corrective applications and change the specific visual content of the picture in ways that cannot be detected. This means being able to make something significantly different, even radically different, from what was captured in the initial exposure. For example, completely altering the size, shape and appearance of a person, or taking out and adding objects or even backgrounds. Such unprecedented options have raised a fundamental question for photographers (and for the **Photography Yearbook** as well), namely, is this, indeed, photography?

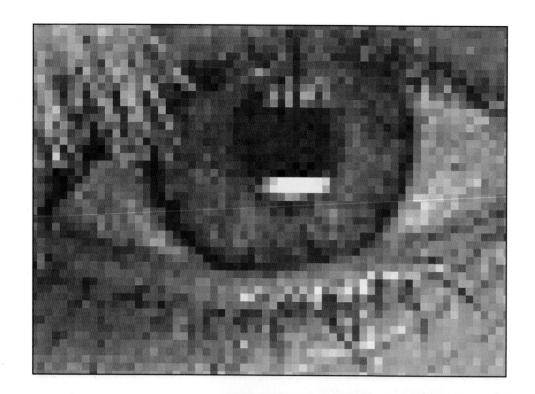

Digital photography is based on the construction of an image from a series of individual picture elements called pixels. In high quality digital images, these pixels are so small and so densely packed that the image looks just like a photograph.
Here, just the eye section of a full head portrait of a woman captured on a small digital file of 2mb has been greatly enlarged so that it is possible to see the individual pixels which appear as squares.
(Colour Laser print)

Most photographers welcome the ability of electronic photography to repair and restore damaged prints and films. In this photograph parts of a scratch that had originally extended across the whole picture have been restored at selected points to show the before and after effects on one picture.
(Thermal Dye Transfer print)

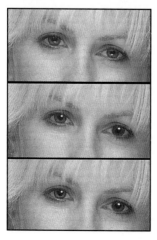

(Photographs by Joseph Meehan)

Very small points can be changed as well such as the alteration of catch lights in the eye and even eye colour.
(Colour Laser print)

Electronic methods also permit the alteration of large parts of a scene as in the removal of the vignetting in the corners of this seascape as shown above. (Thermal Dye Transfer print)

ELECTRONIC IMAGING: PHOTOGRAPHY OR ELECTRONIC ART?

For most of us, the answer to the question: 'Is electronic imaging really photography?' will be based, to a large degree, on how this new technology is perceived. Those deeply wedded to the processes and procedures of silver halide photochemistry often see electronic imaging as a tangible threat on many levels. For these photographers, many of whom have spent a lifetime of passion and love with the processes and materials of silver halide photography, there is the not unfounded fear that electronic image making will soon replace their way of making pictures. It is probably fair to say that these photographers view traditional photographic materials as almost magical in the way they capture light and translate it into pictures. For them, the flicker of a computer screen with its total control of the image with every keystroke is little more than a video game with no place for the mystery of the alchemist's hard earned skills.

There is also a general apprehension amongst these photographers about the authenticity of the photograph in the future. This is based on the fact that the analog capture of reality all at once with conventional photochemical processes, will be replaced by a technology in which 'everything is possible in the computer and therefore nothing is real'. That by relying on the computer's ability to change the image, the photographer is no longer remaining faithful to the original subject. That what traditional photographers have learned to do in the darkroom with burning and dodging and with filters when taking the picture was merely refining what was there. But, digital imaging too often produces something that wasn't there in the first place. Consequently, photographs which have been 'significantly altered electronically' should carry some sort of symbol to indicate that fact, less they be accepted as 'authentic photography'.

Some have further suggested that electronically manipulated images not be considered photography at all and, therefore, cannot take a place under the hard won banner of 'photography as art'. Instead, such images should be considered a separate form entirely; perhaps as electronic art. Ironically, this viewpoint is somewhat reminiscent of those 19th century portrait painters, who proclaimed the death of painting with the appearance of the first Daguerreotypes, predicting that photography would never be considered art.

This issue of authenticity has also been taken up by others who are less concerned with preserving traditional photographic methods, but are very sensitive to the questions of how correctly the photograph reflects reality. These are people who have to rely on photography, for example, in legal applications as in insurance and criminal documentation, or in news reporting. Others, mostly photographers, have expressed grave concerns with the potential loss of control the photographer is more likely to experience when selling his or her photographs for publication since this technology makes change so easy by anyone who knows how to use the software. Most of the concerns here boil down to one question; how far should treatment by the new technology be applied before the photograph is no longer considered a valid representation of the subject?

We do not have to think very long about these concerns before important questions are raised such as: 'Can we continue to rely on the use of photographs as evidence or for documentation without some sort of method or system of certification?' 'How much protection is provided to prevent a photographer's work from being manipulated by a stock or advertising buyer?' 'If several photographs are combined together (with the photographer's permission), who is the owner of the new image?' 'And what of the whole genre of nature photography were the premise is that the photographer is capturing subjects in their natural setting?'

So, it appears that even without dealing with the question of whether or not digital imaging is 'really photography' and the philosophical or emotional issues that it stirs up, this new technology is now and will continue to cause an upheaval in the way societies perceive and use photographs.

One hundred and eighty degrees removed from these views are those photographers who see the new media as a way of extending one's creativity and that it is simply another method of making photographs with endless possibilities of expression. These proponents point out that the equipment they use are just tools; what counts is the picture and what it says to the viewer. Furthermore, electronic photography removes much of the tedious methods and environmentally undesirable procedures and materials associated with photochemical processes. That this new form of photography represents a new era with new opportunities for expression.

Eventually, they say, society will work out the legal questions that have been raised as has happened with all new technologies. Much of the criticism about whether digital imaging is true photography comes from people who are not familiar with the new technologies and want to preserve only what they are used to working with. Furthermore, if their objections to digital are also strictly applied to many conventional photographic practices, they would eliminate such methods as hand painting black-and-white photographs, especially in those cases where the colours are selected that were not in the original scene. And then there are procedures such as solarization, sandwiching, double and multiple exposures, tinting of monochrome prints and even extreme cases of burning where parts of the photograph are eliminated. And what of the results of slower shutter speeds that produce blurs in the motion of individuals that are never perceived by the human eye. Thus, to deny electronic photography its rightful place on the grounds that it is 'not the correct technology' is to deny opportunities for creativity and the tide of progress itself. Saying that photographs must be made with photochemicals is tantamount to restricting music to acoustical instruments and overlooks the fact that electronic and photochemical forms of image making can coexist as in movies and television.

WHAT DOES THE FUTURE HOLD FOR PHOTOGRAPHY?

Hundreds of articles and many books have been written, speculating about whether the relationship 'between the old and the new will be one of coexistence or replacement, as well as considering other ways in which the new technology will impact on photographers and society in general. The most balanced of these writings have rightly seen that we are, today, in a period of transition between these two forms of image making and that the answers about the future of photography (electronic or traditional) are far from clear.

We know, for example, that many companies have invested great sums of money to develop better and more sophisticated electronic based imaging products while, at the same time, traditional photographic products, from new films to view cameras to enlargers, continue to appear in an unabated stream and in far more sophisticated forms. It is also true that the early grandiose predictions of an irresistible tide of electronic imaging in which we would all be toting 'electroflexs', has not even begun to happen. And yet, every day we hear of new and better scanners, digital cameras, computers and photo imaging software, all of which appear to be fulfilling the promise of the superiority of the digital image and its irresistible attraction to many photographers. It is, needless to say, a confusing time for all photographers, amateur and professional alike, as they grapple with trying to decide how these changes will impact on them.

There is varied opinion among experts as well, including those who are producing photographic products. For example, Eastman Kodak's CEO, George Fisher, who heads the world's largest producer of photographic film and paper as well as being a leader in digital imaging, was asked this year at a news conference if he saw the replacement of silver halide films and papers with digital technology? "I don't see digital ever fully replacing silver. Silver-based images will continue to increase in numbers for years to come." Commentaries in most of the established photographic magazines also seem to see at least an extended period of coexistence between the old and the new technologies. This is a reversal of those early confident declarations in advertising for digital products that film's days were numbered and the new wave of photography was digital, a position also taken by some photo writers who, early on, climbed wholeheartedly onto the digital band wagon.

Thus, the idea that if you did not go digital as soon as possible you would be left behind, has given way to the co-existence view as represented by a recent editorial in the *British Journal of Photography:* "Silver halide and electronic processing do not necessarily conflict with each other as they are both concerned with producing an image." British writer, Geoffrey Crawley also pointed out that the perceived differences between digital and conventional photography should be looked at in a more balanced way. That is, "the same laws of optics, lighting, perspective and so on apply to any means of recording an image- one is just using a different tool."

Nevertheless, there are certain inescapable forces at work as Dave Howard, Executive Editor of *Camera and Darkroom* magazine in the United States points out; "In this increasingly overcrowded and polluted world, any largely chemical-dependent process that can be minimized or eliminated will ultimately benefit the environment. While I think film and paper supplies for hobbyists and fine-artists, though steadily dwindling in variety, will continue to be available for some time, I think the ultimate desertion will gradually set in as more imaging artists experience the flexibility, incredible creative options, lack of waste, and operational cleanliness of the digital realm. For the traditionalist fretting about the prospect of change, keep in mind that

digital imaging can be done in black-and-white, too! Time and technologies change, and, eventually, so do photographers."

Most observers agree that the digital tide seems to be strongest in professional photography, particularly those concerned with any form of publishing, in part, because that industry has been using advanced computer systems for some time. Just how the professional will be effected has been summarized by photographer, writer, and teacher, George Schaub. He is Editorial Director of the Photo Group of PTN Publishing, the largest trade publishing group in the world whose many publications serve equipment manufacturers, photo retailers and professional photographers. "The profound change wrought by the way in which professional photographers make pictures - from capture to manipulation to output - and in the way images are brought to page with direct to plate technology has and will create the same disruption that accompanies any technological shift. As of 1995, this has resulted in both starting imagery and a virtual tower of visual babble.
Until standardization is instituted, and most publishers have the capabilities to handle the picture information supplied on disk, there will be a good degree of wasted effort and time on everyone's part. 95% of all images will still be recorded on film into the year 2000, with commercial photography and photojournalism feeling the shift first. After that, for professionals at least, all silver halide bets are off."

Paul Wenham–Clarke
Flowers in Piano
The piano was shot on location and the flowers were shot separately in the studio and then the two were comped together on the Quantel Graphic Paintbox.
Client: Quantel - Newbury Spring Festival Poster.

Paul Wenham–Clarke
Spring, Summer, Autumn, Winter
Industrial abrasive products photographed for a calendar, in a series of four. The subject was lightpainted with Microfield Scientific's 'Lightbrush 300' and won a Gold Award at the British Institute of Professional Photography's 1994 National Print Competition.
Concept: Paul Wenham-Clarke.
Client: 3M U.K. PLC. Abrasives Division.
Camera: 5x4 Monorail Horseman L45. Lens: 180mm.
Film: Fuji Velvia.

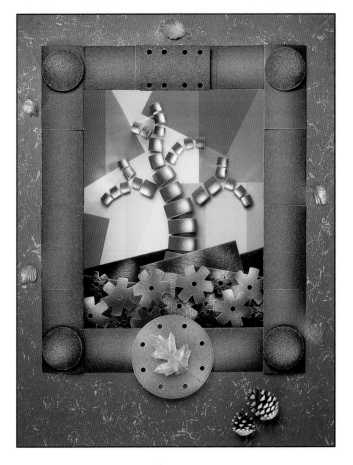

ELECTRONIC PHOTOGRAPHY AND THE PHOTOGRAPHY YEARBOOK

Since the **Photography Yearbook's** mission is to chronicle the best of photography each year and we would expect to receive electronic based images in our submissions, there is an obligation on our part to make clear a position on this whole subject. Perhaps the most obvious option is to simply separate electronic and traditional images in our presentation, but there are serious implications to this approach. First of all, there is no fair way to determine which pictures have, in fact, been treated electronically and manipulated in some way. And if to anticipate this, photographers were required to stipulate any digital treatments as part of their submissions, that would immediately single out these images and beg the question: "Why not require all photographers to indicate which images were filtered or had extensive burning and dodging, or were reproduced using various copy methods?"

It appears obvious to us that taking a position on electronic imaging cannot come as a result of such procedural responses to submissions. Indeed, our stand on this matter must come from the answer to the larger question raised by this revolution: "Is electronic imaging photography?" Our answer is that photography is first, last and always about two things; light and content. About what is being said by the photograph and how light was used to produce it. About the decision of the photographer to place within his or her frame, certain visual elements which merge together to form a statement. In our selections we look for those pictures that make such statements in some extraordinary way so as to merit inclusion in the **Photography Yearbook.**

We sympathize with photographers who have laboured perhaps their whole lives to attain a particular level of understanding of the silver halide processes and see electronic approaches as an unacceptable way to make photographs. Yet, it must also be pointed out that photography cannot be defined by a particular process, but rather by its most basic definition as 'the capture of a subject in a moment of light'. Or as it is more completely put forth in the 1993 *Focal Encyclopedia of Photography* (3rd Edition): "An image of one or more objects produced by the chemical action of light or other forms of radiant energy on sensitized materials. By extension, an image formed by an electronic imaging system (electronic photography)."

It is therefore our conclusion that photography does not belong solely to any particular light sensitive media or technology, any more than it belongs to any particular style or the rules set up by any photographic organization. It belongs to those who take pictures by whatever means of recording they chose. Over its 61 years of existence, the **Photography Yearbook** has published pictures reflecting changes in subject matter, style and, yes, different treatments such as multiple exposure, image sandwiches, solarization, filter use, special films and a host of non-silver forms of photography. At one time there was even a section called "Experimental Photography" the existence of which presumably meant that they encouraged photographers to experiment. Since the primary mission of the Yearbook is to present a cross-section of photography, we cannot exclude or separate by category, any process that is used to produce those photographs.

Whether it was taken by a very sophisticated autofocus SLR, a beautiful wooden view-camera with a legendary lens, a simple snapshot camera or created in its final form later in the darkroom or the computer, it is still a picture made up of light and content. The only exception to not separating out different media in the book's presentation would occur when a specific photo-process is featured. For example, as part of special coverage in order to explain the fine points of that process as we are doing this year with electronic photography.

We do feel, however, that readers of the **Photography Yearbook** would like to know something about how the images were made. Therefore, we will be asking photographers to supply information such as camera type, film, lens exposure and any other pertinent information that they think would help the readers understand how the picture was produced. The Yearbook has had a long history of supplying such information and we will be making an effort to expand this in the future. We see this as a good practice since there are now so many different ways to effect the final image, both through traditional and electronic processes, that supplying such information would be of definite educational value to the reader.

Finally, it is worth pointing out that the revolution in electronic imaging has had one effect that can only be seen as beneficial. It has caused all photographers to more critically examine what they consider the essence of photography and, in the end, that should be the most universal benefit of this revolution. We at the Yearbook hope that photographers will use the changes being brought about by electronic photography as an opportunity to examine and perhaps re-define the reasons why they have chosen to be photographers and understand more completely, what the making of a photograph means to them.

(1) The term 'imaging,' is being used here to refer to pictures produced by either electronic or photochemical means since there has been no agreement as yet to receive this term only for electronically generated pictures.

PAUL WENHAM-CLARKE - PAINTING WITH LIGHT

Paul Wenham-Clarke is the photographer responsible for the images featured in this special feature.
Paul is 31 years old and is a commercial / advertising photographer based in Reading, Berkshire, England where he works with his partner Gianna Tognarelli ABIPP, together they form In Camera. Paul has become well known for his creative studio photography involving model making and special lighting effects . In much of his work Paul has conceived the original ideas as well as producing the final photography.

In recent years he has used light painting to enhance his images and has become an expert at using this technique. The camera lens is opened with the room in complete darkness and using a very powerful fibre optic light (the lightbrush) the image is slowly built up as the photographer moves around the set lighting objects one at a time. The result can look almost like an illustration if very little conventional flash lighting is used. The concepts for the Quantel cards and the four lightpainted images that were produced as a seasonal calendar for 3M Abrasives on page 19 were all original ideas of Paul's. The photographs for 3M were especially challenging as the frame to each image and everything inside the frame are abrasive products, even down to the colour of the 'sky' in each shot. Deciding what each image represented and which products fitted the mood of each shot took as long as building the set and lightpainting it.

One of Paul's clients is Quantel, the manufacturer of the Graphic Paintbox and Printbox. Utilising this equipment has allowed Paul to develop his style further, combining lightpainting with electronic manipulation. This amazing combination of lightbrush and Paintbox meant that ideas that were once totally impractical are now

very easily possible. This is especially apparent in the way live animals appear in Paul's lightpainted images, a particularly difficult subject to photograph normally as animals are not noted for their ability to sit still in the dark while you shine a powerful light at them! Apart from rabbits! Now there's an idea. Many of the Quantel assignments allow Paul and Gianna to use their imaginations to the full and as a result these projects probably produce their best work.

"My philosophy on photography is literally to have the freedom to capture images that are in your mind, it does not matter to me how this is done whether it is by using film or electronic devices is irrelevant. You might say why not paint these images as surreal artists such as Rene Magritte did, but you only have to look at his work to see that he painted in a way that is very realistic, or even photographic. It makes you wonder how he would have produced his images today, with a camera and a Paintbox possibly? Some of my work has been criticised for appearing as if it were an illustration but my answer is, who is to say where photography stops and illustration starts? Why should we care anyway, as its the image that counts! In this era of electronic manipulation the boundaries between the different fields of art are undoubtedly blurring but this is not a bad thing as it is allowing photographers and artists to reach their full potential with no fences to hold them back.
Here's to the future!

Paul Wenham-Clarke
Produced from seven separate transparencies and compiled in the Quantel Graphic Paintbox for Quantel's 1994 Christmas card. The owl and the mice in the shots are all live animals. The grandfather clock is not a model, it was a real antique, 7ft tall. Six of the separate images are studio shots and the seventh, the shot of the wood was shot on location in Bracknell. Parts of some of the images were lightpainted with Microfield Scientific's Lightbrush 300.

Concept Paul Wenham-Clarke. Client: Quantel - Quantel Christmas Card. Camera: 5x4 Monorail Horseman L45. Lens: 180mm. Film: Fuji Velvia.

THE PORTFOLIOS

IN PAST YEARS, THE PHOTOGRAPHY YEARBOOK regularly reserved a substantial number of pages for the work of a few individual photographers.
In this "Portfolio Section," we are returning to that popular practice with the work of five outstanding photographers from around the world. The main reason for reviving this practice is that a portfolio of work gives the viewer a more complete picture of the photographer's vision as it relates to the subject and is therefore likely to give the reader a better understanding of that photographer's work in general.

So here, in the opening pages of this 61st edition of the Photography Yearbook, are the photographs of five talented photographers. While they may be from very different parts of the world and their motivation, subjects, style and vision are very different, all have one thing in common; they have all produced striking images that make us stop, look and think about what the photographer has done with the camera.

Miloslav
STIBOR

AND THE MOTION OF THE FEMALE FORM

EW PHOTOGRAPHERS would argue with the statement that the human form, and the nude in particular, is a very popular subject for photographers, but one that is difficult to carry out so as to attract a wide audience of admirers. While there are many reasons why an audience may or may not respond to a nude photograph, photographers must focus themselves on one basic question: "What characteristics of the human form are to be brought out in the photograph and how is this to be accomplished?" For Miloslav Stibor of the Czech Republic, the answer has been to combine the line and curve of the human form with a sense of motion to produce the ethereal representations that flow across the following pages.

A retired Professor of Art at the Palachky University (Olomouc) and a past Director of the Olomouc Art College, Stibor began photography in the 1950's as a vocation and eventually perfected a unique style of presentation that combines natural and studio strobe light. During the communist regime in the former Czechoslovakia, the depiction of the human form was a limited area for expression given the artistic restrictions that were in place. And yet, Stibor's work was so appealing, with its strong classic overtones and dream-like qualities, that he was eventually able to exhibit widely in his own country and in more than 100 exhibitions in Europe. He was also the first Czech artist to exhibit such work in the USSR. *"For the regime, I was something of an ambassador for Czechoslovakia as I exhibited my works all over the world."*

Stibor has actually gone through several phases in his photography in which he would concentrate on a particular approach, always in the studio and always with non-professional models. *"In the early days, I saw my nudes as static and very geometric, often as a visualization of exact mathematical and geometric principles."* The more free-wheeling representations we see here began to take shape in the mid-1970's and were produced, in part, through the use of a special strobe arrangement that would fire the unit into an umbrella in the middle of a longer available light exposure, usually in the quarter to eighth of a second range. In the end, he succeeded in combining the symmetrical lines of the human form with a sense of motion transcribed through the flowing movements of the hair and clothing; all rendered in the printing process with a softness of detail that finalizes his exquisite representation.

GIBELAE 80-1990

PELLITÀ 17-1988

TENERITÀS 2-1989

TERPSICHORE 21-1976

Martyn Colbeck

Photograph by Cynthia Moss

MANY PHOTOGRAPHERS HAVE tried dividing their professional efforts between cinematography and still photography only to find such a dichotomy to be a difficult undertaking at best. For although there are many similarities between these two forms of image making, there are also significant and challenging distinctions. Perhaps the most defining of these is the fact that the still frame has four sides that clearly set the limits to the composition while the frame of the motion picture can move in any direction during the recording of an image. One of those who has succeeded in adapting to such differences is Great Britain's Martyn Colbeck. He is a freelance film-maker now working almost entirely with the BBC Natural History Unit all over the world making films for television. But he has always had a love of the still picture and the subject that finally allowed him to merge his cinematographic and photographic skills is an animal whose survival in the wild remains an open question; the free ranging African elephant.

Colbeck refers to these intriguing animals as "very special", a phrase that does not completely describe his deep concern for them as living creatures and obvious fascination as photographic subjects. It was whilst working on

the filming of the David Attenborough television series 'The Trials of Life' for the BBC that Colbeck first met "the animals that were to have a significant effect on my life". During that project, he also met and worked with Cynthia Moss, Director of the Amboseli Elephant Research Project, who has studied the elephants of southern Kenya's Amboseli National Park for almost 25 years.

Shortly thereafter, Colbeck worked again with Moss on a film which was based on a simple but remarkable premise; to follow the same family of elephants and document everything they did for a two-year period. The outcome of this extraordinary project was the film, 'Echo of the Elephants' and a book of the same title based on Colbeck's still images. This very successful undertaking was followed by an even more intense study of the same family which lasted four years resulting in a new film to be released early in 1996.

The images you see here are from the six years Colbeck has spent in what can only be called an intensive, intimate and, indeed, familial relationship with these majestic animals. His respect and love of the elephant is as much part of the extraordinary images on the following pages as is his prodigious technical skill at capturing on to a single frame of film, revealing moments in their behaviour.

This 35 year-old bull elephant, named Mr. Nick because of the numerous nicks and tears out of his ears, came to within a couple of feet of me as I lay on the ground beneath a Land-Rover enabling me to take this photograph on a 20mm lens. All the elephants in the Amboseli population have been named by Cynthia Moss, who for over 20 years has directed the Amboseli Elephant Research Project - the longest continuous study of individually known elephants in Africa.

During periods of heightened sexual activity, or 'musth' as it is called, adult bull elephants secrete temporin from the enlarged temporal glands just behind their eyes. During musth some bulls become aggressive but this one, Sleepy, remained approachable.

I unexpectedly came across Sleepy dusting shortly after dawn one morning in 1992. I knew immediately that the situation had great potential. Sleepy repeatedly blew huge quantities of dust over his head. As he emerged from the clouds of dust I took several pictures. The previous frame to this one won me the Wildlife Photographer of the Year award in 1993. Sadly Sleepy disappeared two years after this photograph was taken. It is thought likely that he was shot by trophy hunters when he crossed the border into Tanzania.

When elephants have enough to eat and feel safe they often indulge in play sessions. This four month old calf rushed headlong through the tall elephant grass before stopping, lifting his head high and looking for the next imaginary enemy to attack.

Calves are born into the secure and highly social world of the elephant family. This calf is being looked after by its older sister. These so-called allomothers take on many of the responsibilities of caring for the calves when they're not with their mothers.

Very few elephant births have ever been seen in the wild let alone photographed. I was lucky that the whole family gathered behind the new-born calf allowing me unrestricted views as it struggled to free itself of the birth sac. The mother, Brita, bent down to help it while the rest of the family celebrated the new calf's arrival with a deafening chorus of rumbling and trumpeting. Within 15 minutes the new calf was walking, albeit with diffculty. Each step was carefully monitored by the family members who were ready to help it back to its feet should it fall over.

Elephant calves love to climb on each other. Here an older member of the family is trying sleep but its prostrate body proves irresistible to the younger calf.

The key to the Amboseli ecosystem is its central swamps which attract wildlife in abundance including wildebeest, buffalo, zebra, oryx and elephants. The water comes via underground aquifers from the slopes of Kilimanjaro, which at 19,340 ft is the tallest free-standing mountain in the world.

Male elephants leave the family around the age of 14. They then form loose associations with other adult bulls and spend large portions of the year in favoured bull areas. However during their musth phase males search over vast areas for receptive females.

As the sun rises and the elephants move towards the life-giving swamps during the dry season they pause occasionally to dig roots from the dusty ground. Their outlines frequently become indistinct as plumes of fine alkaline dust engulf them.

During the dry season the central swamps are the only source of water for the animals in Amboseli. The edge of this swamp, Enkongo Narok, is a favourite place for a number of families and knowing this I was able to lie in wait beneath the Land-Rover for them to arrive. Despite being within a few feet of the elephants as they slaked their thirst they were unaffected by my presence.

In order to document the lives of our chosen family of elephants, the EBs, we needed their trust. Here one of the matriarchs' daughters looks down at me as I lay on the ground just a few feet from where she stood. It is difficult to describe what it feels like to be trusted in this way by a wild animal.

Elephants mudwallow regularly. The glutinous mud cools their bodies and coats the skin in a layer of natural suntan lotion. This particular wallow was a perfect consistency - neither too wet nor too dry. It was at times like this that I felt a desperate urge to put my cameras aside and participate in what looked like heaven-on-earth.

Elephant families are led by the oldest female, the matriarch. This female, Jezebel, was a great favourite of all the Amboseli researchers before she died of natural causes in November 1993. She was estimated to have been in her late fifties.

Gentle sparring serves to reinforce bonds between elephants as well as giving young males the opportunity to test each other's strength.

45

After Jezebel, the matriarch of the JA family died the leadership was taken over by another female, Joyce. It is thought that Joyce may be Jezebel's sister. It is the matriarchs of the families that are the repositories of knowledge for their families and for the population as a whole.

Lillian, named after Cynthia Moss' mother, is one
of the oldest elephants in the Amboseli population as
well as one of the most predictable. Her home range
is very limited and she can usually be found feeding
in the central Longinye swamp. On this particular
evening early in the rainy season the most intense
rainbow I have ever seen arched above Lillian as she
stood bathed in the rays of the setting sun. I had
waited over five years for all the elements in these
photographs to come together - black sky, rainbow,
low evening light and elephants.

All the photographs in this portfolio were taken on
Fujichrome Velvia film using Canon EOS-1
cameras and 20-35mm F2.8L, 28-80mm F2.8-
F4, 80-200mm F2.8L and 300mm F2.8L lenses.

All photographs copyright
Martyn Colbeck / Oxford Scientific Films

Pedro Luis RAOTA

A PASSION FOR THE IMAGE

TEN YEARS AGO THIS YEAR, on March 4, 1986, Pedro Luis Raota died of cancer at the age of 51 after a career in photography so full of international awards that the editor of Hasselblad-Zeitschrift described him as "the world's most successful photographer in this respect." He was born in Argentina into a farm family and as a young man began the study of law. The story goes, that he became intrigued with

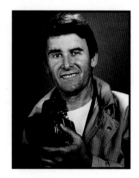

photography and soon launched himself completely into this profession. According to his wife, Claudia, "he found that one can fly and dream with the camera" and this ability to create scenes of life and then record them with technical precision became his passion.

Raota, who became one of his country's best known personalities, seems to have been intent on using every moment of his photography to say something to the viewer. To make statements that were clear and perfect in their arrangement and yet appeared spontaneous in their occurrence. He was proud of his "humble origin" and of having learned his profession "from the streets," so, not surprisingly, much of his imagery reflects many common, day-to-day themes. Again, in the words of his wife; "he taught us to know quite everyday scenes in a new and intensive way and to make contact with people through photography."

Each Raota photograph is a statement about life that focuses attention on a specific theme as represented through the people he has chosen and the setting as well as the way he prints them in the darkroom, using developers he modified himself. There is no confusion about his point and no question about what he has presented; be it the portrayal of an emotion or the contrast between social forces.

That he held an intense passion for his images, for his life's work in photography, is best illustrated by the last days of his life. When he learned in December 1989, that he had an incurable cancer, Raota devoted what turned out to be his remaining weeks to work in his darkroom, printing his images right to the day he had to enter the hospital were he died 24 hours later.

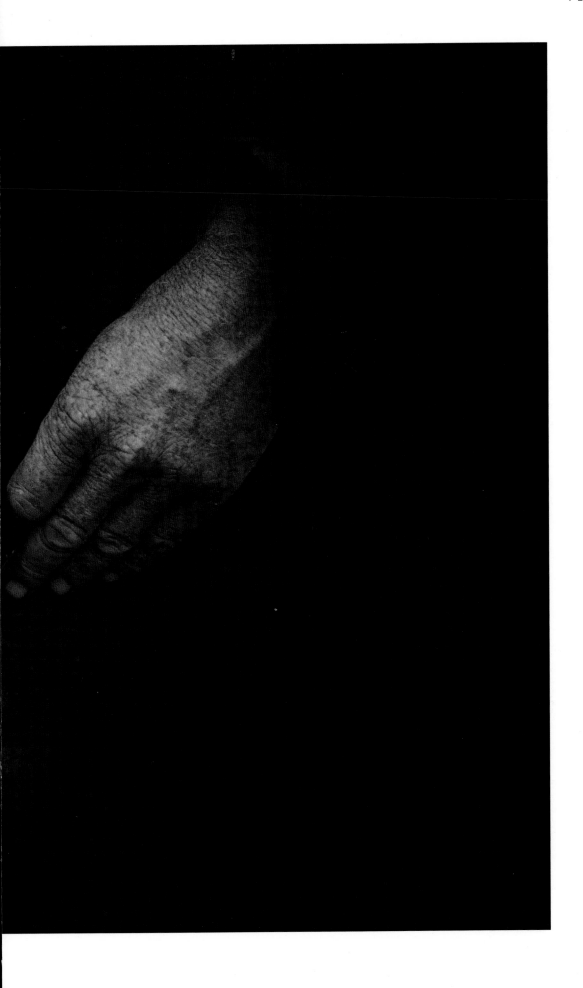

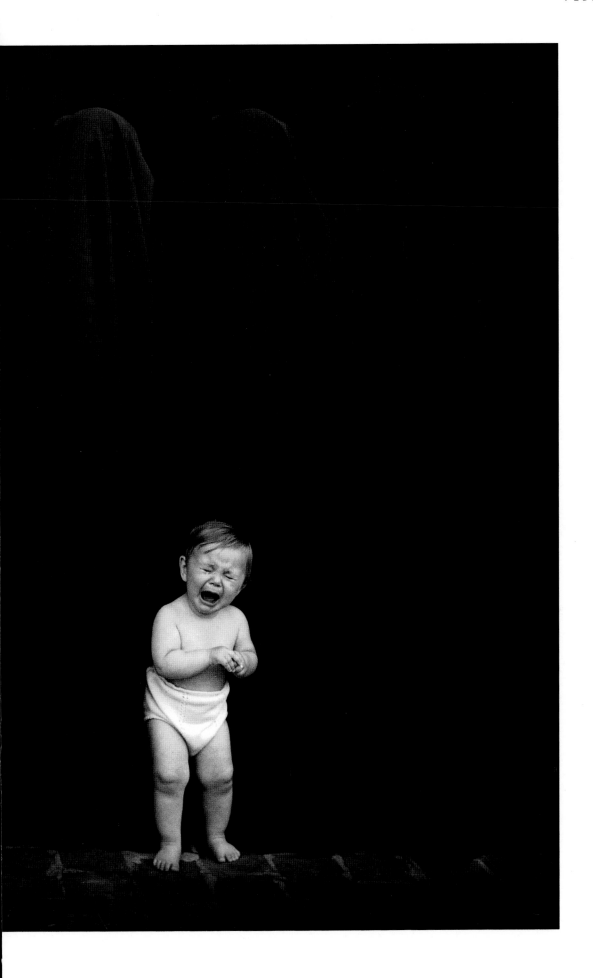

ROBERT FARBER
AMERICAN MASTER OF THE COMMERCIAL IMAGE

ROBERT FARBER WORKS IN A WORLD WHERE EGOS reign supreme, where photography exists to establish an image and where to survive, a photographer must combine a mind for business with a personality to handle the temperamental, to say nothing of the unexpected. This is a world in which the selection of a model with "just that look" and finding the "perfect location" may take weeks of preparation and thousands of dollars in costs. And where everything comes down to the photographer being able to produce that one picture that encapsulates everything a small army of art directors, stylists, advertising executives and models have been working for.

Obviously, this is not a place for those insecure in their work, timid in their approach, nor is it for anyone who thinks that commercial photography is about having the right equipment and a big studio to use it in. On the contrary, it is about being talented and knowing how to use that talent in a world notorious for paying great attention to "hot" new talents, only to then suddenly drop them into instant obscurity.

Robert Farber's long and successful career, that began in the 1970's, is at least due in part to his early realization that he had to produce something that was more than the mere execution of the art director's sketch. His style has been described as a beautiful combination of sensuality, fantasy and mystery, often with a strong reliance on texture in the presentation of the subject. "Farber's work is as much a painting done with light as it is the capture of light," which is quite appropriate since Robert Farber has always looked to the great painters (especially the Flemish masters) for his inspiration. His work, with its strong overtones of fine art photography, also has enormous appeal outside the commercial world as shown in the popularity of his many books which are now approaching the 400,000 total sales mark worldwide. The beautifully illustrated "Classic Farber Nudes" published by Amphoto Books, New York, is the current best seller of this American Master Photographer.

VLADIMIR VITOV

PHOTOGRAPHY AT THE EXTREME

Photography is often used to document the lives and culture of a group of people, capturing as it does, the details of life for us to study and contemplate. Such a result, however, requires a photographer who not only understands his subject, but can capture its most important qualities on film. Just the briefest look at the photographs on the next few pages recording the lives of Northern Europe's Lapp reindeer herders, will reveal that Vladimir Vitov has, indeed, done just that. This type of photography, taken under sub-zero temperatures, is often called "photography at the extreme," and perhaps there is no better phrase to summarize Vitov's general working conditions of extreme cold, limited light and the physical dangers of being within herds of wild animals.

Vladimir Vitov is a retired military photographer who now lives in St. Petersburg, Russia. He spent virtually his whole career in the former Soviet armed forces stationed in Murmansk, in Northern Russia. While there, he devoted much of his free time to photographing the Lapps, using a Zenit SLR and a Horizont panoramic camera. In these extraordinary pictures he has captured for us to see, and almost feel, the stark expanse of the land and the swirling danger of working the wild herds. But there is also the singular intensity of the people seen in the faces of the panoramic images and perhaps ultimately symbolized by the casual protrusion of the cigarette from the mouth of the herdsman engulfed by the motion of the herd.

Vitov's pictures are not merely documentations, but powerful representations that capture the raw relationships between man, animal and the land; all living together in the most marginal of interdependent relationships. The grainy texture and blurred motion reflects, in part, the light conditions of an area of the world that sees the sun for only portions of the year as well as Vitov's own limited access to photographic materials to produce this highly personal work. But while he may have had to work at the extreme with limited resources, there is no limit to the impact of his dramatic images and what they tell us of the lives of these people.

INTERNATIONAL GALLERY

Dung-Leung Lin

HONG KONG

John Philpott

UNITED KINGDOM

88

Enrico Patacca

ITALY

Alberto Porres

SPAIN

Mike Hollist

UNITED KINGDOM

Jose Arias
SPAIN

Walter Hintermaier

AUSTRIA

Heather Urquhart

UNITED KINGDOM

Rosemary Calvert

UNITED KINGDOM

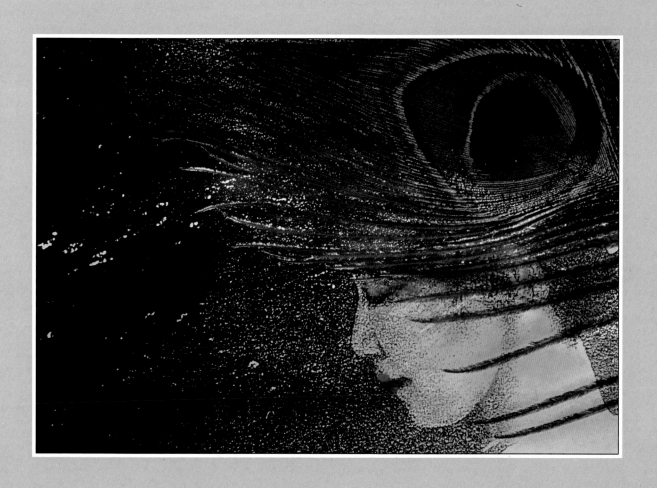

W. Plohberger

AUSTRIA

Peter Kittel

GERMANY

Uschi Stuart

SOUTH AFRICA

Barbara Nash

UNITED KINGDOM

Andreas Friedmann
AUSTRIA

Mike Travers

UNITED KINGDOM

Joerg Arenz

GERMANY

Mike Hollist

UNITED KINGDOM

Mike Hollist

UNITED KINGDOM

111

Brian Tuff
UNITED KINGDOM

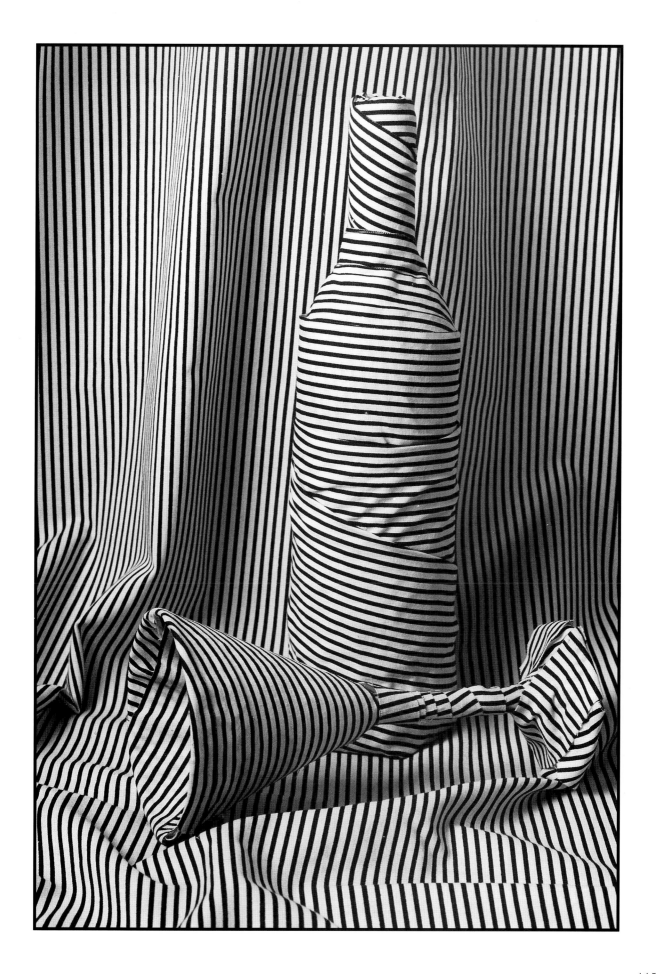

115

Ueli Leuenberger

SWITZERLAND

Werner Halm

GERMANY

117

Andrzej Krynicki

POLAND

Tony Worobiec
UNITED KINGDOM

Klaus Schidniogrotzki
GERMANY

121

Marcel Ritschel

AUSTRALIA

122

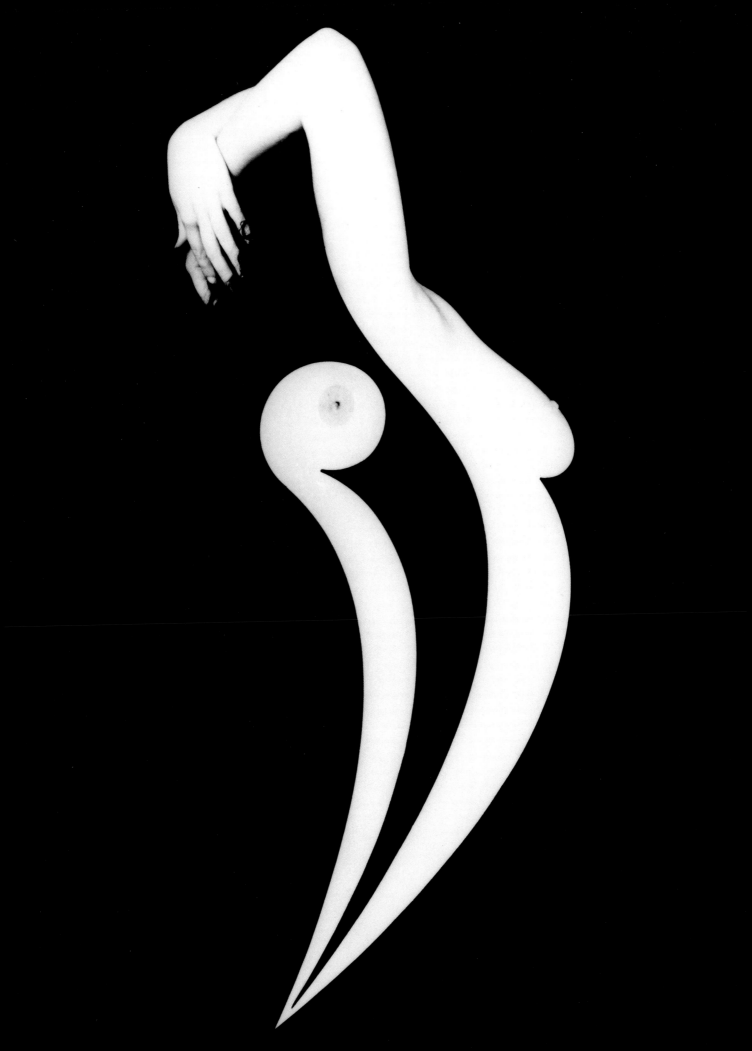

Uschi Stuart
SOUTH AFRICA

Werner Halm

GERMANY

Azam Adnan

PAKISTAN

128

Cyril Mazansky

UNITED STATES

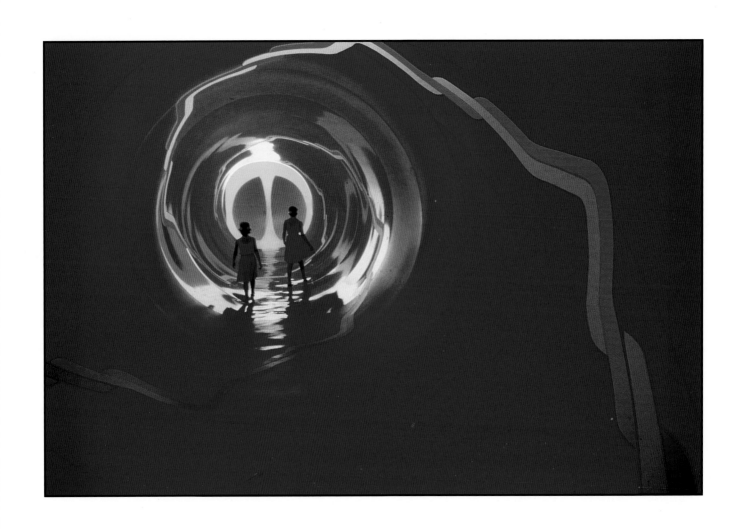

Jim Hartje
UNITED KINGDOM

130

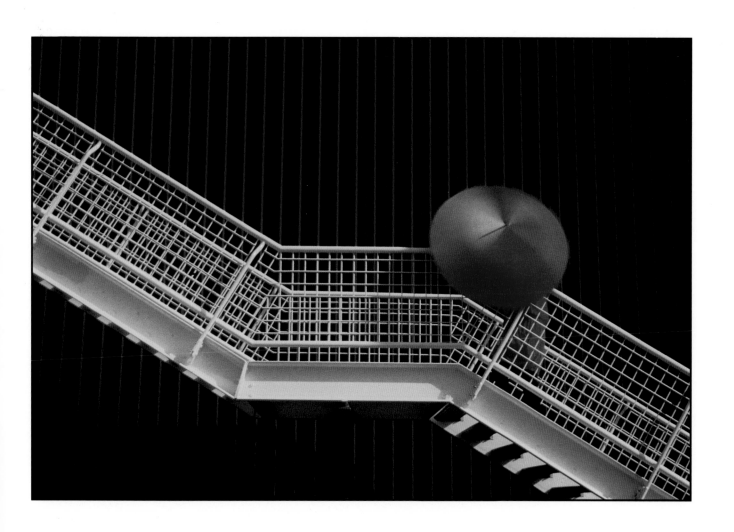

Eckhard Schultz
GERMANY

131

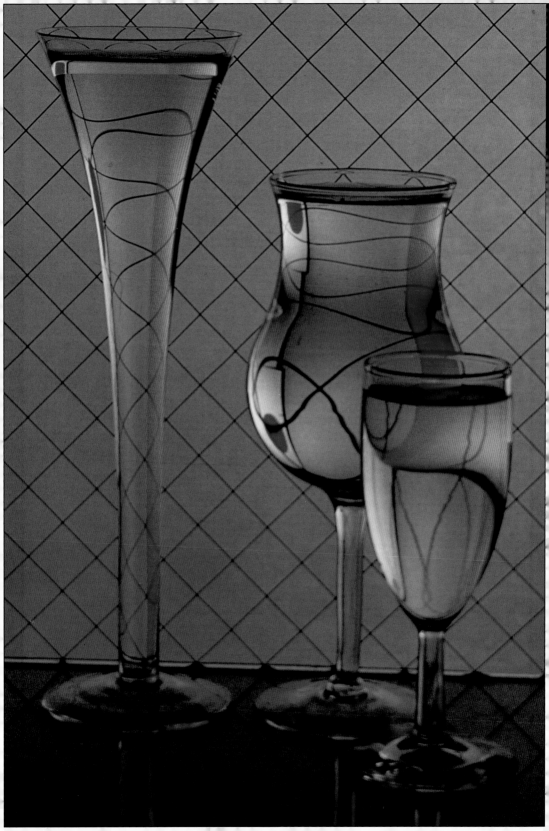

Claudio Calvani

ITALY

Sue Bennett

UNITED KINGDOM

Jan de Rycke
BELGIUM

Darren Maybury

UNITED KINGDOM

Carolyn Bates
UNITED KINGDOM

Aphra Bremner
UNITED KINGDOM

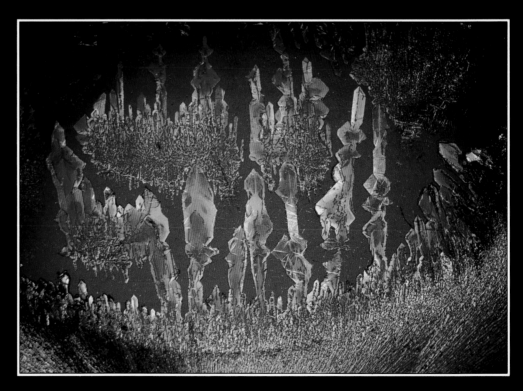

Verner Mogensen

DENMARK

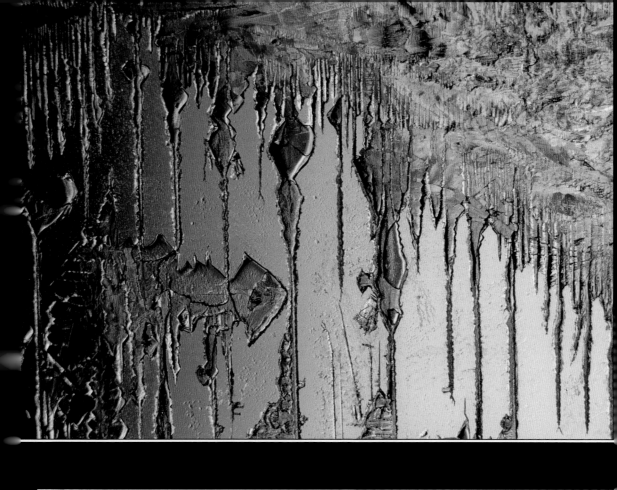

Sergey Buslenko
UKRAINE

144

Keith Vaughan
CANADA

146

Altons Vlaminchx
BELGIUM

Alastair McNaughton
AUSTRALIA

Ian Mellor

UNITED KINGDOM

Alexander Suprun

UKRAINE

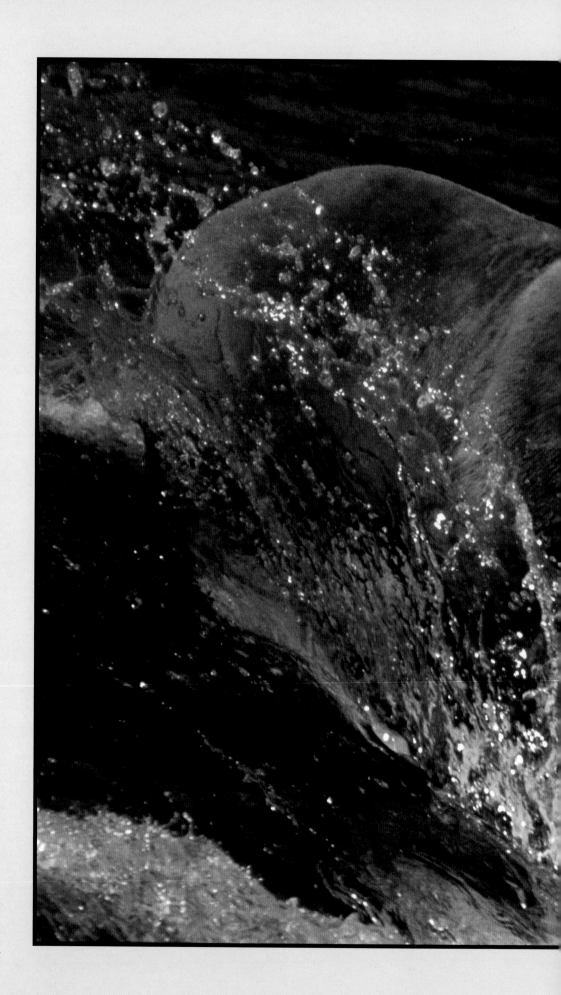

Janis Gleizds

LATVIA

Elsi Hedström

GERMANY

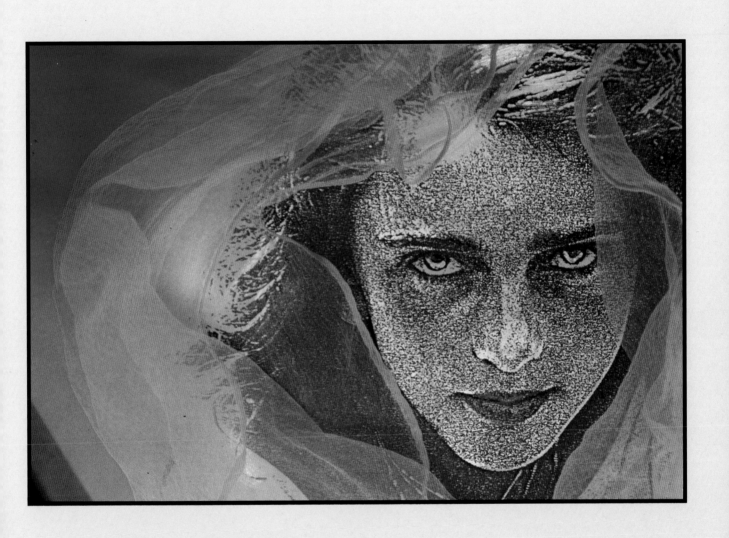

Roger de Groof
BELGIUM

Tony Worobiec

UNITED KINGDOM

Neil Humphries
UNITED KINGDOM

Konrad Funk

GERMANY

172

Colin Harrison
UNITED KINGDOM

Werner Halm

GERMANY

Linda Pitkin

UNITED KINGDOM

Eileen Gamble

UNITED KINGDOM

Vicente Peiro

SPAIN

Klaus Schidniogrotzski
GERMANY

Andrew Foley

UNITED KINGDOM

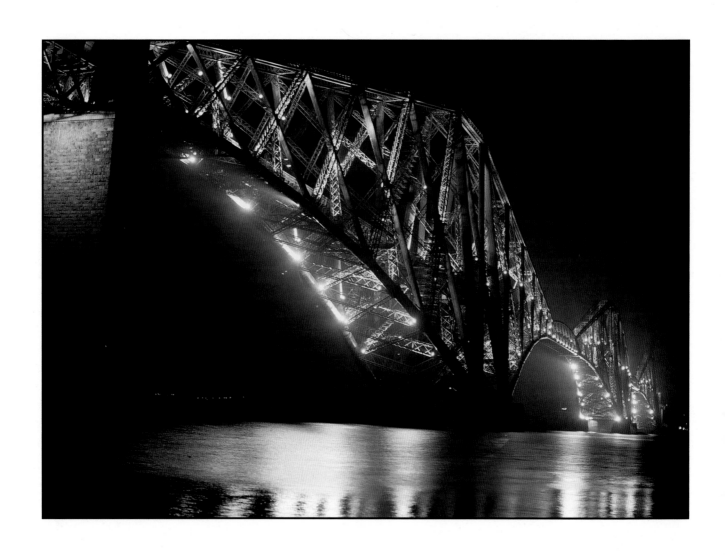

Roger Reynolds
UNITED KINGDOM

John Gray

UNITED KINGDOM

Marcel van Balken
NETHERLANDS

Xaver Klaussner

GERMANY

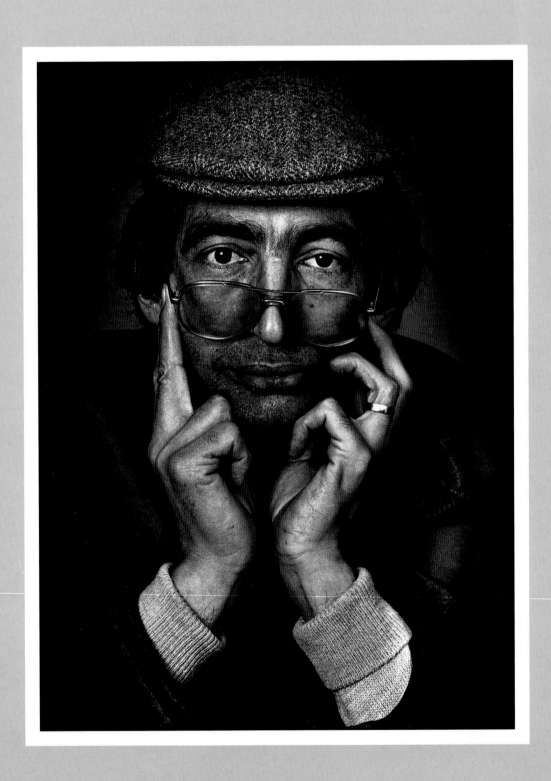

John Philpott
UNITED KINGDOM

198

Koo Stark

UNITED KINGDOM

Joe Camilleri

MALTA

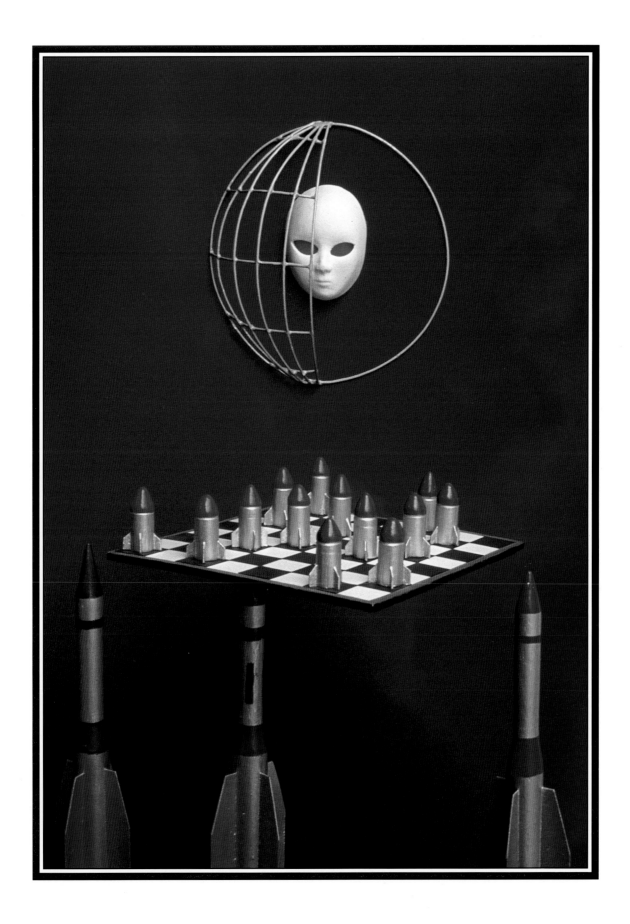

Jukka Salonen
FINLAND

Flor Huyers

BELGIUM

Tom Richardson
UNITED KINGDOM

212

Ian Mellor

UNITED KINGDOM

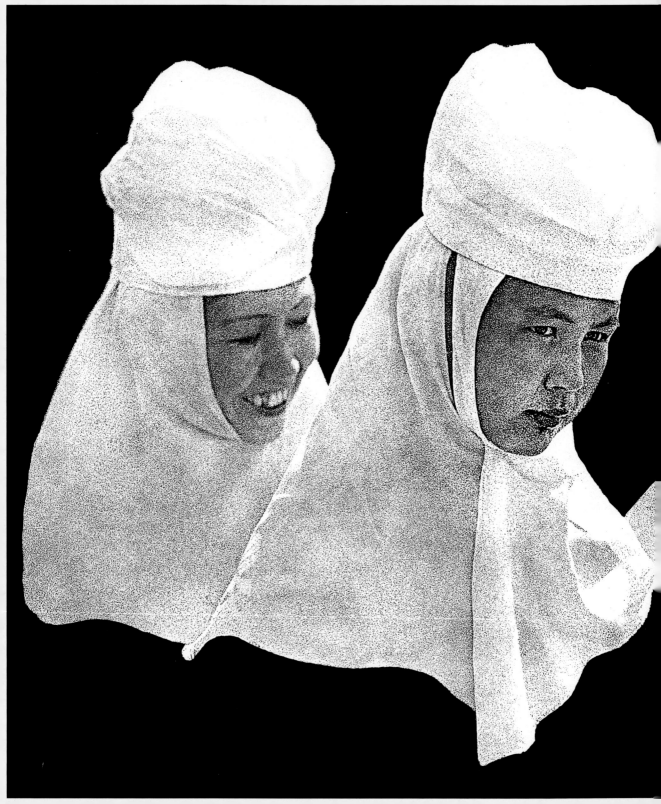

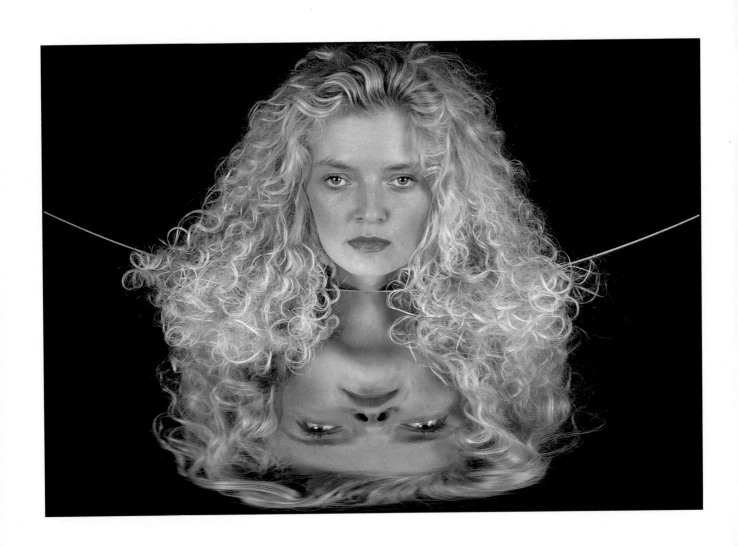

Chris Hinterobermaier

AUSTRIA

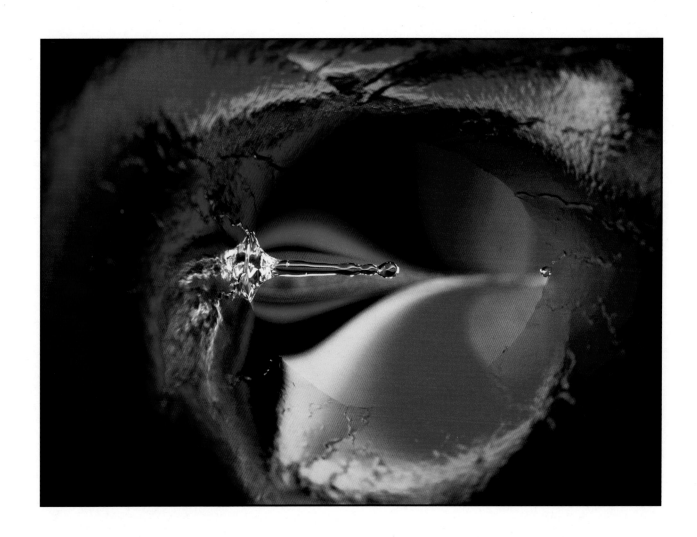

Xaver Klaussner

GERMANY

Tony Worobiec
UNITED KINGDOM

224

REACH FOR THE SKIES!

Photograph by NICKOLAS MURAY

FROM THE RPS COLLECTION

Set your sights on photography - enlist with the RPS! Broaden your horizons- learn many new aspects of photography from the historical to digital imaging. Gain flying colours by trying for one of the Society's Distinctions, which are recognised internationally as evidence of your achievement. Success earns you the right to use the letters LRPS, ARPS, or FRPS after your name.

When you become a member you are encouraged to meet and learn with a wide network of fellow photographers and to take part in the many workshops, lectures, master-classes and informal meetings. Enjoy visits to the world famous Society headquarters based in Bath where you will have unlimited free entry to the five galleries that show an exciting and varied programme of exhibitions. Keep up to date with the informative monthly magazine full of the latest photographic news and views, which wings its way directly to your home, and also includes the lively programme of events.

The Royal Photographic Society

PATRON: HER MAJESTY THE QUEEN

THE OCTAGON, MILSOM STREET, BATH, BA1 1DN

IF YOU ARE WILD ON PHOTOGRAPHY...

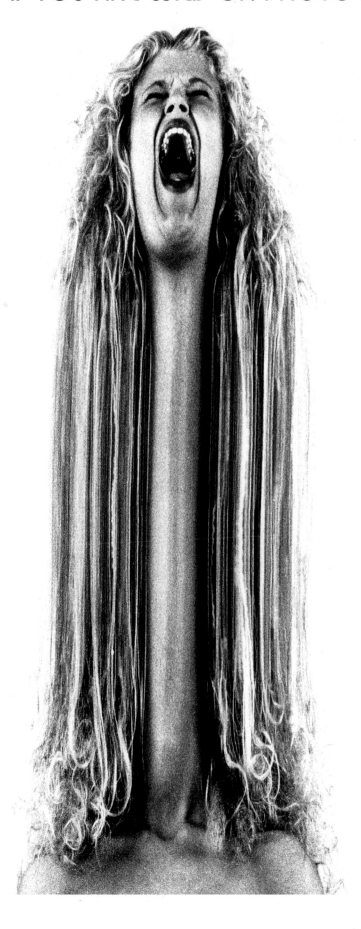

...then we are your partner!

AUSTRIAN SUPER CIRCUIT 1997
sponsored by

the world's largest annual
salon of photography,
recognized by FIAP & PSA!

380 prestigious awards including
a *HASSELBLAD 503 Cxi* and
cash money awards of US$ 15.000!!!

And a 220 page catalogue with more than
300 reproductions for every entrant.

So if you are wild on photography of any
style, technique or theme...

...then don't miss our closing date:
4th of August 1997.

Requests for entry forms and mailing
adress for prints/slides:

AUSTRIAN SUPER CIRCUIT
Postfach 364
A-4010 Linz/AUSTRIA
or fax to:
Austria 732 750100